Black, Gangster, & Respe‹
By Jonah Sanders

While every precaution has been taken in the preparation of this book, the publisher assumes no responsibility for errors or omissions, or for damages resulting from the use of the information contained herein.

BLACK, GANGSTER, & RESPECTED: THE LARRY HOOVER STORY

First edition. January 31, 2025.

Copyright © 2025 Jonah Sanders.

ISBN: 979-8230157663

Written by Jonah Sanders.

Table of Contents

Introduction 1
Chapter 1: Beginnings of a Leader 2
Chapter 2: The Rise of Gangster Disciples 4
Chapter 3: Power in the Streets 7
Chapter 4: Crime and Control 9
Chapter 5: The Murder of William Young 12
Chapter 6: Running an Empire from Prison 15
Chapter 7: Growth & Development Movement 19
Chapter 8: Law Enforcement Crackdown 24
Chapter 9: The Myth and Reality of Larry Hoover 28
Chapter 10: The Gangster Disciples Today 32
Chapter 11: Calls For Freedom 37
Chapter 12: The Politics of Gang Leadership 41
Chapter 13: Hoover's Influence on the Next Generation ... 45
Chapter 14: What If? 50
Chapter 15: Legacy of a Street General 55

Introduction

Black, Gangster, and Respected: The Larry Hoover Story explores the tumultuous life of one of America's most notorious figures—the founder of the Gangster Disciples. From his beginnings as a troubled youth in Chicago to becoming the leader of a criminal empire, Larry Hoover's story is one of ambition, survival, and the complexities of power in the streets. But it is also a story of transformation.

Imprisoned for decades, Hoover has used his time behind bars to rethink his past and shift his focus from crime to community development. Through his Growth and Development movement, Hoover advocates for a life of discipline, reform, and positive change, proving that even the most hardened criminals can evolve and contribute to society.

In this gripping account, we delve into Hoover's rise to power, the violence that defined his empire, the law enforcement crackdown that led to his imprisonment, and his ongoing efforts to redeem himself. The book critically examines Hoover's legacy, questioning what defines a man—his past or his ability to change. With a compelling mix of street-level reality and a look at the personal evolution of a notorious figure, Black, Gangster, and Respected is a must-read for those interested in the intersections of crime, power, rehabilitation, and redemption.

This is more than the story of a gangster—it's a conversation about the potential for rehabilitation and growth, challenging readers to rethink the narratives of crime and punishment.

Chapter 1: Beginnings of a Leader

Larry Hoover's story begins in a place far removed from the streets of Chicago, where he would later become one of the most influential and controversial figures in gang history. Born on November 30, 1950, in Jackson, Mississippi, Hoover was raised in the segregated South, a place where racial tension and economic disparity shaped the lives of Black families.

At the age of four, Hoover's family made the move to Chicago, like many Black families during the Great Migration. The city promised better opportunities, but for young Hoover, it was a world filled with struggle and survival. His family settled on the South Side, a place known for its vibrant Black culture but also for its deep-rooted gang presence.

A Young Hustler in the Streets

By the time he was 12 years old, Hoover was already drawn to the streets. Like many kids growing up in poverty-stricken neighborhoods, he found himself pulled into street life, running with older boys who introduced him to the underworld. It wasn't just about crime—it was about power, respect, and survival.

Hoover became affiliated with the Supreme Gangsters, a small gang operating in Englewood. He quickly stood out, not just for his toughness but for his ability to organize and lead. While other kids were fighting over street corners, Hoover was already thinking about the bigger picture—how to unify and build something greater.

Early Leadership & Rise in the Ranks

As a teenager, Hoover wasn't just another gang member; he was a strategist. He understood that brute force alone wouldn't win battles—it was about numbers, alliances, and influence. By the late 1960s, he had risen through the ranks of the Supreme Gangsters, and his vision for expansion was clear.

But the South Side was a battlefield, and multiple gangs were fighting for control. One of the most powerful organizations was the Black Disciples, led by David Barksdale. Instead of constant war, Hoover saw an opportunity. He proposed unity.

The Birth of a Movement

In a move that changed Chicago's gang landscape, Hoover merged the Supreme Gangsters with the Black Disciples, forming what became known as the Black Gangster Disciple Nation (BGDN). This wasn't just about street control—it was about building an empire.

By his early twenties, Hoover was no longer just a gang member—he was a leader. His influence stretched beyond his immediate neighborhood, and his vision was becoming clearer. But with power came enemies, and the choices he made would soon lead him down a path of no return.

Chapter 2: The Rise of Gangster Disciples

By the early 1970s, Larry Hoover had established himself as a dominant figure in Chicago's gang landscape. His leadership within the Black Gangster Disciple Nation (BGDN) had solidified his reputation as both a strategist and an enforcer. The organization, born from the merger of the Supreme Gangsters and the Black Disciples, was growing rapidly, fueled by a mix of discipline, street knowledge, and criminal enterprise.

Building an Empire

Hoover understood that true power didn't just come from violence—it came from structure. Unlike other street gangs that operated in chaos, he worked to turn the BGDN into a well-organized network. The group had a hierarchical leadership structure, modeled after corporate organizations, where each member had a role and responsibility.

Expansion was key. Under Hoover's direction, the Gangster Disciples spread beyond the South Side, reaching into different parts of Chicago and other Midwestern cities. The organization built a massive membership, recruiting young men from impoverished communities who saw the GDs as both protection and opportunity.

The Code of the Streets

To maintain order, Hoover introduced a set of rules and principles that governed how members operated. These codes emphasized:

Loyalty to the Nation – Betrayal was met with swift consequences.

Respect & Discipline – Every member had a role and was expected to follow orders.

Growth & Power – Expanding influence was just as important as maintaining control.

Symbols, hand signs, and literature were also developed to solidify the group's identity. The infamous six-point star, representing concepts like love, life, loyalty, knowledge, wisdom, and understanding, became a key emblem of the Gangster Disciples.

The Money Machine

With power came business opportunities, and Hoover saw the drug trade as a way to generate revenue. Under his leadership, the GDs became heavily involved in narcotics distribution, controlling key territories in Chicago. The profits funded the expansion of the gang, buying weapons, recruiting new members, and maintaining loyalty.

The gang also dabbled in legitimate businesses, using front organizations to launder money and create a sense of legitimacy. Community centers, youth programs, and charity efforts were sometimes used as a cover for gang operations.

Conflict & Internal Struggles

Despite Hoover's ability to organize and expand, violence was still a constant reality. Rivalries with gangs like the Vice Lords, Latin Kings, and the Black P. Stones led to bloody conflicts across Chicago. Even within the Gangster Disciples, internal power struggles began to emerge as different factions sought control over lucrative drug operations.

One of the biggest challenges came from David Barksdale's leadership of the Black Disciples. Though the two men had united their organizations under the BGDN, their leadership styles and visions often clashed. When Barksdale died in 1974, the unity of the organization started to unravel. Eventually, the Black Disciples and the Gangster Disciples split into separate factions, though the GDs remained one of the most powerful gangs in Chicago.

The Fall Begins

By the mid-1970s, Hoover had built the Gangster Disciples into an empire, but law enforcement was watching closely. His leadership made him a prime target, and his involvement in organized crime was becoming impossible to ignore.

Everything changed in 1973, when Hoover was linked to the murder of William "Pooky" Young, a gang member accused of stealing from the organization. This crime would mark the beginning of Hoover's downfall, setting off a chain of events that would lead to his imprisonment.

The foundation of the Gangster Disciples had been set, but Hoover's influence was about to shift from the streets to behind prison walls.

Chapter 3: Power in the Streets

By the mid-1970s, Larry Hoover had solidified his status as one of the most powerful figures in Chicago's underworld. Under his leadership, the Gangster Disciples (GDs) had grown into a well-structured and disciplined organization, commanding thousands of members and controlling significant territories across the city. Despite internal conflicts and rivalries with other gangs, Hoover's ability to strategize, organize, and lead kept the GDs at the top of the food chain.

Expanding the Organization

Hoover understood that power wasn't just about having soldiers on the street—it was about building an empire that could sustain itself. He continued to push for expansion, recruiting young men from impoverished neighborhoods, offering them a sense of belonging, protection, and financial opportunities.

The GDs weren't just a gang; they operated like a corporation, with a structured hierarchy that included:

Regents – High-ranking members who oversaw entire regions.

Governors – Leaders who controlled specific territories.

Enforcers – Individuals responsible for discipline and carrying out orders.

Soldiers – Foot soldiers who handled drug sales, protection, and gang activities.

This structure allowed the GDs to run street operations efficiently, ensuring that their money, influence, and power continued to grow.

Dominating the Drug Trade

By the late 1970s and early 1980s, the drug trade had become the gang's primary source of income. The heroin and cocaine boom hit Chicago hard, and the GDs took full advantage. With a tight grip on distribution networks, the organization pulled in millions of dollars, using the profits to fund its operations, expand into new territories, and strengthen its infrastructure.

Hoover's leadership meant that violence was strategic, not reckless. While street battles were unavoidable, the GDs operated with a level of discipline that set them apart from other gangs. They weren't just fighting for territory; they were running a business.

Influence Beyond Chicago

With the money came expansion. The GDs spread beyond Chicago, establishing a presence in cities across the Midwest and even reaching into the South. The organization's influence extended into prisons, where GD members maintained control over drug smuggling, protection rackets, and recruitment efforts.

As the GDs grew, law enforcement began to take notice. The FBI and Chicago police launched task forces dedicated to dismantling the organization, recognizing that Hoover's influence extended far beyond the walls of any prison or street corner.

The Community & The Image of Power

Despite their involvement in crime, the GDs also worked to build an image of community leadership. Hoover encouraged members to invest in their neighborhoods, funding community programs, organizing food drives, and advocating for political influence. This duality—criminal enterprise mixed with community outreach—helped the GDs maintain a level of public support, even as law enforcement cracked down on their activities.

Hoover's ability to maintain power from behind bars would soon take center stage, proving that his influence was greater than anyone could have imagined.

Chapter 4: Crime and Control

As the Gangster Disciples (GDs) expanded in the late 1970s and early 1980s, their power was deeply rooted in organized crime and structured leadership. Larry Hoover, even behind bars, maintained an iron grip on the gang's operations, dictating orders that influenced both the streets and the prison system. His control over the GDs wasn't just about fear—it was about strategy, discipline, and maintaining a balance between crime and control.

The Criminal Empire

The GDs' criminal activities were widespread, covering everything from:

Drug trafficking – Controlling the distribution of heroin, cocaine, and crack across Chicago and beyond.

Extortion – Running protection rackets in both the streets and inside prison walls.

Weapons trafficking – Smuggling and distributing illegal firearms.

Fraud & money laundering – Using legitimate businesses and front organizations to clean drug money.

Hoover ensured that the gang functioned like a corporation, with different crews handling specific operations. He set up a system where members paid "street taxes"—a portion of their earnings—to the gang's leadership in exchange for protection and rank within the organization.

Maintaining Order Through Fear & Loyalty

The Gangster Disciples thrived because of their strict code of conduct. Hoover implemented rules that every member had to follow, enforcing discipline with severe consequences for those who disobeyed.

Snitching was punishable by death.

Disrespecting leadership resulted in severe beatings or worse.

Stealing from the organization meant execution.
Loyalty and secrecy were non-negotiable.

This code kept the GDs strong. Members who betrayed the organization faced immediate retaliation, ensuring that the fear of Hoover's reach extended far beyond his prison cell.

Controlling the Streets from Prison

Despite being locked up for the 1973 murder of William "Pooky" Young, Hoover's influence never wavered. If anything, his imprisonment made him even more powerful. Through a network of trusted lieutenants, he issued orders from behind bars, controlling everything from gang wars to business dealings.

Hoover's ability to communicate with outside leadership was key to maintaining control. He used coded messages, legal visits, and intermediaries to continue running the GDs as if he were still on the streets.

Inside prison, he built alliances with other inmates, ensuring that the GDs had a stronghold behind bars as well. His ability to merge criminal enterprises with prison politics made him one of the most powerful incarcerated figures in the country.

Law Enforcement Takes Notice

By the late 1980s, the rise of crack cocaine and escalating gang violence had placed the Gangster Disciples at the center of Chicago's crime crisis. Law enforcement agencies, including the FBI and the DEA, stepped up efforts to dismantle the organization.

The government began using RICO (Racketeer Influenced and Corrupt Organizations Act) charges to target gang leaders who were orchestrating crimes from behind bars. Hoover was already serving a 150- to 200-year sentence for murder, but federal authorities were determined to bring him down further.

With law enforcement closing in, Hoover would soon attempt a dramatic shift in his public image, hoping to outmaneuver the system that was trying to break him.

Chapter 5: The Murder of William Young

In 1973, the murder of William "Pooky" Young became a pivotal moment in Larry Hoover's rise to power and his eventual downfall. This event would not only shape the trajectory of Hoover's leadership within the Gangster Disciples but also serve as the catalyst for his long-term imprisonment. The crime, and the aftermath, brought Hoover into direct conflict with law enforcement, setting in motion a series of events that would drastically alter the course of his life and the future of the GDs.

The Context of the Murder

William Young, known on the streets as "Pooky", was a gang member within the Gangster Disciples. His involvement with the GDs had given him some level of respect, but his actions would eventually lead to his downfall. Hoover's leadership within the gang was built on discipline, loyalty, and order, and Young's behavior challenged that structure.

At the time, the Gangster Disciples had established strict rules and a code of conduct that governed their criminal activities. Disloyalty, stealing, and betraying the organization were considered cardinal sins. Hoover took a hardline stance on discipline, enforcing these rules with extreme measures. Young had reportedly stolen money from the gang, an act Hoover viewed as a direct challenge to his authority and the integrity of the organization.

Hoover's Decision

When Hoover learned that Young had stolen from the Gangster Disciples, he saw this as an unforgivable act of betrayal. In Hoover's eyes, betrayal wasn't just a personal insult—it threatened the stability of the entire organization. Loyalty was everything, and those who crossed that line had to face the consequences. Hoover, known for his cold and calculating nature, ordered Young's execution as a clear message to anyone who might consider betraying the gang.

The decision to have Young murdered was a stark illustration of Hoover's leadership style—ruthless and uncompromising. Under his rule, members who violated the gang's code were dealt with swiftly and without mercy.

The Murder

In a calculated and brutal act of violence, Young was lured to a location where he was executed. The exact details surrounding the murder remain unclear, but it was widely believed that Hoover personally gave the order for Young's death. While the killing was framed as a lesson for the rest of the gang, it would come back to haunt Hoover in the form of legal and moral ramifications.

The murder set off a chain of events that would become a significant chapter in the Gangster Disciples' history, highlighting Hoover's willingness to enforce the gang's code at any cost. It also marked the beginning of the end for Hoover's reign as an untouchable leader in the streets of Chicago.

The Aftermath

The murder of William Young did not go unnoticed. Law enforcement quickly took an interest in the case, suspecting that the Gangster Disciples were behind the crime. Hoover's direct involvement in the killing became evident, and it wasn't long before authorities began building a case against him.

However, Hoover's control over the gang didn't waver. He remained a powerful figure, not just on the streets but also in the prison system. While law enforcement tightened their grip on the GDs, Hoover's leadership continued to resonate with his followers. His discipline-based approach to managing the gang kept the organization united, even as the pressure from outside forces mounted.

Though Hoover would later claim that the murder was necessary to maintain the integrity of the Gangster Disciples, it became a defining moment in his legacy—both as a leader of one of Chicago's most notorious gangs and as a man whose pursuit of power would eventually lead him to a life behind bars. The murder of William Young set the stage for Hoover's conviction and his eventual rise to infamy in the history of American gang culture.

Chapter 6: Running an Empire from Prison

Despite his imprisonment, Larry Hoover's influence over the Gangster Disciples (GDs) remained unparalleled. In 1973, Hoover was convicted for the murder of William "Pooky" Young and sentenced to a 150 to 200-year prison term. Yet, far from being a setback, his incarceration marked the beginning of his most powerful phase. From behind bars, Hoover would continue to run a sprawling criminal empire, controlling the GDs with unmatched authority and efficiency. His ability to command loyalty, maintain operations, and manipulate events from his cell would cement his reputation as one of the most influential incarcerated figures in U.S. history.

Establishing Control from Within the Prison System

Larry Hoover's first few years in prison could have been a time of vulnerability. However, his innate understanding of power dynamics, combined with his organized approach to leadership, ensured that he quickly established dominance in the prison system. Hoover knew that prison life was often harsh, violent, and chaotic, but he used this to his advantage, creating a structure that mirrored the discipline and order he had maintained on the streets.

He established a network of trusted lieutenants and enforcers inside the prison who would carry out his orders. By tapping into the prison system's hierarchical structure, Hoover was able to position his allies in positions of power, such as in prison gang factions and other inmate organizations, which gave him leverage to control the movement of goods, drugs, and weapons.

Through this network, Hoover maintained contact with key Gangster Disciple operatives on the streets. Even though he was physically incarcerated, his reach extended far beyond prison walls—his power was felt in Chicago, across the Midwest, and in cities where the GDs had established themselves.

Communication: The Art of Staying Connected

One of Hoover's most impressive feats was his ability to communicate orders, strategies, and decisions despite being in a maximum-security prison. To circumvent the physical and legal barriers that should have limited his ability to control the gang, Hoover employed a range of covert methods:

Intermediaries: Trusted GD members from the outside world acted as couriers to relay Hoover's messages to street-level operatives.

Letters and Codes: Hoover used coded language in letters to avoid interception by law enforcement. The codes were often simple yet effective, enabling him to maintain control over operations without raising suspicion.

Prison Visits: Legal visits and family visits allowed Hoover to pass on instructions to his key members in person, providing a direct line of communication to the outside world.

The "Street Tax" System: Hoover set up a "street tax" system for GD members on the outside, ensuring that his control over the organization was financially maintained. This system ensured that a portion of profits from drug dealing, extortion, and other illicit activities went directly into Hoover's hands.

The Gangster Disciples Expand Further

Despite being confined to a prison cell, Hoover's reach continued to grow. The Gangster Disciples expanded beyond Chicago, increasing their territories in cities like Atlanta, Detroit, New York, and even California. The gang's operations were vast, ranging from drug trafficking, money laundering, extortion, and illegal gambling. Hoover's strategic leadership kept the GDs one step ahead of law enforcement and rival gangs, allowing them to expand their influence across the nation.

Hoover's transformation into a symbol of power in the underworld was no accident. His ability to manipulate the gang's resources, manage conflicts, and impose order in chaos made the GDs a well-organized, efficient criminal enterprise.

Maintaining Discipline and Loyalty

Inside prison, Hoover continued to emphasize the importance of discipline and loyalty—values that had been central to his leadership since the beginning. To ensure compliance, Hoover used fear and respect in equal measure. Members who violated the gang's rules were swiftly dealt with, and any attempts to undermine Hoover's leadership were met with harsh retaliation.

Hoover's leadership was built on more than just criminal activity; it was about maintaining a sense of identity for his followers. He preached the importance of loyalty to the gang and the necessity of a brotherhood built on shared interests. His influence extended into prisons, where GD members were positioned in such a way that the gang's power continued to grow.

A Shift in Public Image

Over time, Hoover's strategy began to shift. He recognized that his public image, both within the prison system and outside, was crucial to maintaining his empire. In the 1980s, Hoover began to present himself less as a violent street boss and more as a community leader.

Hoover sought to reposition the Gangster Disciples as an organization dedicated to community empowerment and upliftment. In prison, he started the "Growth and Development" philosophy, encouraging GD members to embrace education, business practices, and positive community change. While this was largely seen as a rhetorical shift designed to appeal to those who were considering leaving the street life, it was also part of Hoover's attempt to position himself as more than just a criminal kingpin.

The development of the Growth and Development ideology would influence the direction of the GDs for years to come, even as the organization's criminal activities continued unabated.

Legal Challenges and Federal Scrutiny

As Hoover's empire continued to grow, so did the government's efforts to bring him down. Hoover's ability to operate his organization from prison became a major concern for law enforcement, especially as his influence seemed to reach new heights. The RICO Act (Racketeer Influenced and Corrupt Organizations Act) became a tool used by the government to target organized crime leaders like Hoover.

In the mid-1980s, the FBI began investigating Hoover more intensely, suspecting that he was still heavily involved in the criminal operations of the GDs, despite his incarceration. Law enforcement efforts to cut off the gang's communication network, seize assets, and disrupt operations became more aggressive. Yet, Hoover's ability to stay one step ahead of these efforts was a testament to his resourcefulness and unyielding control.

Legacy of an Incarcerated Kingpin

Larry Hoover's ability to run a criminal empire from prison is a testament to his extraordinary leadership skills, adaptability, and understanding of power. While many would have been broken by years behind bars, Hoover's status as leader of the Gangster Disciples only solidified. His influence within the gang, the prison system, and even the broader criminal world is unmatched in modern American history.

Despite his ongoing legal battles and efforts by law enforcement to dismantle his empire, Hoover's legacy as a prison kingpin and street visionary remains entrenched in the world of organized crime and beyond.

Chapter 7: Growth & Development Movement

As Larry Hoover's influence continued to expand within the prison system and the streets, he recognized the necessity for a shift in how the Gangster Disciples (GDs) were perceived, both internally and externally. The Growth and Development (G&D) Movement became Hoover's strategic attempt to rebrand the GDs, emphasizing a new ideology that would help transform the organization's image from one of violence and criminality to one of positive change, self-improvement, and community empowerment. This chapter explores Hoover's creation and promotion of the G&D philosophy, how it impacted the GDs, and its lasting legacy.

The Birth of Growth and Development

The Growth and Development Movement was founded by Hoover in the 1980s while he was incarcerated. Recognizing that his criminal empire was thriving despite his imprisonment, Hoover began to understand that in order to maintain the loyalty of his members and expand his influence even further, the Gangster Disciples needed a new direction—one that spoke to the aspirations of young men in Chicago's underserved communities and beyond.

Initially, Hoover's focus had been on discipline, control, and power. However, as time passed, he saw the potential of offering more to his members, especially those looking for a way out of the dangerous cycle of crime and violence. Hoover's new philosophy called for an emphasis on self-improvement, education, and business development—all concepts that were a significant departure from the gang's roots in street-level crime.

The Growth and Development Movement was about lifting up the individual while still maintaining loyalty to the gang's larger cause. Hoover's message was clear: members could stay loyal to the GDs while also striving for a better future.

Core Principles of Growth and Development

At the heart of Hoover's new movement were several key principles that he believed could help transform not only the Gangster Disciples but also the lives of the men and women within the organization:

1. Self-Growth: The G&D movement emphasized the importance of personal development. Hoover advocated for self-education, self-discipline, and personal responsibility. He saw the street life as a dead-end path and encouraged his followers to pursue more meaningful lives. The movement urged GD members to get involved in positive activities, such as starting businesses, learning trades, and continuing their education.

2. Community Empowerment: Hoover believed in the potential of the Black community to thrive through unity and collective action. He encouraged GD members to focus on helping their communities rather than exploiting them. This meant getting involved in local organizations, helping to fight poverty, unemployment, and crime—the very issues that many GDs had previously contributed to.

3. Economic Independence: One of the key tenets of Growth and Development was the idea of economic empowerment. Hoover recognized that the gang's illegal enterprises could be repurposed to create legitimate business ventures. He urged members to invest in legal industries such as real estate, transportation, and entertainment. By creating wealth within their own communities, Hoover believed GDs could break the cycle of dependence on crime and violence.

4. Non-Violence and Unity: Hoover's philosophy of G&D also emphasized non-violence and unity among GD members. While the

gang had been notorious for its violent actions, Hoover wanted to foster a sense of brotherhood and peace within the organization. He promoted the idea that members should work together towards mutual goals, respecting each other's contributions.

5. Cultural Identity: A significant part of Hoover's Growth and Development philosophy was reclaiming and fostering a strong sense of cultural identity. This was particularly important in the context of the African American community, which had long struggled with systemic racism and social injustice. Hoover's vision for G&D was to empower Black youth, showing them that they could rise above their circumstances through unity, self-discipline, and community involvement.

The Impact on the Gangster Disciples

The introduction of Growth and Development had a profound effect on the GDs. Many of Hoover's followers found the new direction appealing, as it promised a way out of the cycle of violence and crime that had previously defined their lives. It provided a new sense of purpose—something to strive for beyond the streets and gang warfare.

However, not all members of the GDs were immediately receptive to Hoover's new philosophy. Many gang members were entrenched in the old ways of doing things and saw Growth and Development as a betrayal of the gang's roots. Tensions arose within the ranks, as older, more traditional GD members clashed with those who embraced Hoover's vision for change.

Despite this resistance, Hoover's leadership, along with the promise of self-improvement and economic opportunity, helped the Growth and Development movement gain significant traction. Over time, the philosophy became a guiding force for the Gangster Disciples, and many members chose to align themselves with Hoover's vision of creating a better future for themselves and their communities.

Reaching Beyond the Streets

One of Hoover's major achievements with Growth and Development was how he successfully reached beyond the streets. His messages began to resonate with young people who were not involved in the gang but were living in similar circumstances—those who were facing poverty, lack of opportunity, and disillusionment. Hoover's vision for change attracted the attention of youth who had never been involved with the GDs but found inspiration in his message of self-betterment and empowerment.

As a result, the G&D Movement also became a social and cultural force in certain communities, encouraging young people to seek education, start businesses, and get involved in local activism. Hoover, though still incarcerated, became an icon—a figure who was now being viewed not just as a criminal kingpin, but as a leader who could speak to the broader struggles of Black America.

Legal Challenges and the Government's Response

Despite Hoover's efforts to rebrand the Gangster Disciples through the Growth and Development philosophy, law enforcement and the government remained suspicious of the movement's true motives. Many believed that Hoover was using the rhetoric of positive change to conceal his ongoing control over the GDs' criminal enterprises.

As Hoover continued to promote Growth and Development, he faced increased legal scrutiny from law enforcement agencies. Authorities were skeptical of his transformation and continued to monitor his activities both inside and outside the prison. Hoover's rebranding effort was seen by some as an attempt to mitigate the growing pressure from law enforcement, which had been working hard to dismantle his empire.

Legacy of Growth and Development

Although Larry Hoover's Growth and Development movement did not completely eradicate the gang's criminal activities, it left an indelible mark on the Gangster Disciples and broader gang culture. The emphasis on education, self-discipline, and community empowerment offered an alternative vision to the destructive cycles that had previously defined street gangs.

The legacy of Growth and Development also continued to resonate with many former GD members who went on to lead successful lives, start businesses, and give back to their communities. Hoover's ideology, despite its challenges, provided a framework for personal transformation and helped shape the future of many individuals who might have otherwise remained entrenched in criminality.

Ultimately, Growth and Development was Larry Hoover's attempt to leave a positive legacy, proving that even in the most dire circumstances, a person could strive for growth, change, and transformation—not only for themselves but for their community.

Chapter 8: Law Enforcement Crackdown

As the Gangster Disciples (GDs) grew in power and influence, so did the scrutiny from law enforcement. Despite Larry Hoover's push for positive change through the Growth and Development (G&D) Movement, the U.S. government and local authorities remained committed to dismantling Hoover's empire, believing his influence over the GDs was a threat to public order and safety.

This chapter examines the intensified law enforcement actions against Hoover, the GDs, and their criminal enterprises. It highlights the efforts to target Hoover and his associates, both inside and outside the prison system, as well as the broader criminal justice response to the gang's growth and Hoover's attempts at reform.

Increased Law Enforcement Attention

By the mid-1990s, Hoover's efforts to shift the Gangster Disciples from a violent street gang to a more community-oriented organization under the G&D banner was not enough to shield him from the full force of law enforcement. While Hoover promoted self-improvement, education, and community empowerment, the GDs remained heavily involved in criminal enterprises, including drug trafficking, extortion, and violent crimes. Hoover, despite his leadership in the G&D movement, was still seen by authorities as a major player in a vast criminal network.

The federal government, state authorities, and local law enforcement agencies viewed Hoover's influence as a serious threat to their ability to maintain control over Chicago's streets. As a result, a concerted crackdown ensued in an effort to disrupt the Gangster Disciples' operations and undermine Hoover's leadership.

Operation "Cabrini Green" and the Crackdown on the GDs

One of the most high-profile law enforcement operations targeting Hoover and the GDs was Operation Cabrini Green, named after the notorious Cabrini-Green housing projects in Chicago, which were a hotbed of GD activity. This operation, conducted by the FBI, Chicago Police Department, and other local agencies, was designed to dismantle the gang's leadership structure and disrupt their criminal operations.

The crackdown was fueled by Hoover's growing influence, which had spread far beyond Chicago. With the gang involved in various illegal activities, including drug trafficking, money laundering, and weapons offenses, law enforcement viewed Hoover as the central figure behind a criminal enterprise that spanned multiple states.

Authorities argued that Hoover's Growth and Development Movement was merely a smokescreen for his continuing control over the GDs' criminal activities. Despite Hoover's insistence that he was working to change the gang's culture, law enforcement's efforts to suppress the GDs were relentless, and Hoover became an increasingly high-priority target.

Hoover's Conviction and Sentencing

In 1995, after years of investigation, Hoover was convicted of murder, conspiracy, drug trafficking, and a range of other charges related to his leadership in the Gangster Disciples. The charges stemmed from his role in organizing and directing criminal activities, both while incarcerated and during his time outside prison. Hoover was already serving a sentence for a previous 1973 murder conviction, but his new conviction led to a life sentence without the possibility of parole.

One of the most significant aspects of Hoover's conviction was the federal government's claim that he was the leader of a continuing criminal enterprise, a violation under the RICO Act (Racketeer Influenced and Corrupt Organizations Act). The conviction solidified Hoover's status as a major figure in the criminal underworld, and despite his efforts to reshape the GDs, he became an emblem of the state's war on organized crime.

The Role of the RICO Act

The RICO Act, which was passed in 1970, was one of the government's most powerful tools in the fight against organized crime.

By targeting criminal organizations as a whole rather than just individual criminals, the RICO Act allowed authorities to prosecute the leadership and control structure of criminal enterprises. This was particularly relevant in Hoover's case because it enabled authorities to prosecute him not just for individual crimes, but for his role in directing and managing the activities of the GDs across the country.

The RICO prosecution painted Hoover as the mastermind behind a network of criminal operations that profited from drug sales, extortion, and violent crime. Law enforcement argued that his charitable initiatives through Growth and Development were nothing more than a front for his continued criminal activities. As a result, Hoover was sentenced to life in prison, a fate that would see him locked away for the rest of his life, regardless of his efforts to reform.

Targeting Hoover's Influence from Prison

Despite being incarcerated, Hoover's influence within the GDs remained powerful. Prison officials, law enforcement, and the federal government continued to work together to limit his ability to run the gang from behind bars. Hoover's communications with GD members were monitored, and authorities went to great lengths to ensure that his leadership and control over the gang were diminished.

The Bureau of Prisons took extraordinary steps to limit Hoover's ability to communicate with the outside world. He was placed in solitary confinement for extended periods, and his phone calls, letters, and other forms of communication were heavily restricted. Despite these measures, Hoover still found ways to influence his followers, whether through trusted intermediaries or through coded messages.

Law enforcement's crackdown on Hoover's operations also extended to his finances. Federal agents worked to trace and seize the gang's illicit profits, making it harder for Hoover to fund his reform efforts or maintain control over the gang's activities.

The Public Perception of Hoover's Arrest

Hoover's arrest and conviction were met with mixed reactions. Some saw it as a long-awaited victory for law enforcement, an essential step in taking down one of the most dangerous criminals of the modern era. Others viewed it as a sign that the criminal justice system was still unwilling to allow for the possibility of redemption. Hoover's supporters argued that his efforts to promote growth and development should have been taken into account, and that his sentencing was too harsh, given his leadership in attempting to reform the GDs.

For many in the community, Hoover became a symbol of both resilience and oppression. He had sought to transform his gang into something better, but the government's actions reflected an unwillingness to allow this kind of change, viewing his criminal past as too entrenched to overcome.

The Ongoing Struggle Between Reform and Control

The battle between Hoover's vision of Growth and Development and the government's crackdown on his criminal empire continued to play out over the following decades. Hoover's supporters, both inside and outside prison, maintained that he was a force for positive change in the community, while authorities continued to monitor and dismantle any remnants of his control over the GDs.

While Hoover's influence may have been curtailed by his incarceration, the law enforcement crackdown did not erase the ideals behind Growth and Development. Even from his prison cell, Hoover's vision continued to inspire former members and others who were seeking alternatives to a life of crime.

The law enforcement crackdown was a defining chapter in Larry Hoover's story—one that showcased the tension between the state's efforts to suppress criminal organizations and the potential for individuals to change, even within the most oppressive systems. Despite Hoover's incarceration, his legacy of Growth and Development lives on, offering a complex view of reform, redemption, and the lasting power of influence from behind bars.

Chapter 9: The Myth and Reality of Larry Hoover

Larry Hoover's story is one shrouded in both myth and reality, blending the tale of a gang leader who commanded immense respect with that of a man attempting to reform and redefine his legacy. Over the years, Hoover has become a symbol—not only of the criminal underworld but also of the possibility of change and redemption. This chapter delves into the mythic persona of Hoover that has been crafted by both his followers and his detractors, and contrasts it with the reality of his life and actions. By examining these contrasting narratives, we uncover the complexity of Hoover as a figure who was both a product of his environment and someone who sought to transcend it.

The Myth of Larry Hoover: The Kingpin Leader

Larry Hoover's influence, both in the streets and in popular culture, has been legendary. To many of his supporters, he is viewed as a kingpin—a powerful figure who rose from humble beginnings to dominate Chicago's gang scene, establishing the Gangster Disciples as one of the most recognized and influential gangs in the United States. To some, Hoover became more than just a gang leader; he became a symbol of resilience, someone who could transcend the constraints of his environment and shape the future of the gang in a way that would benefit those under his influence.

The myth of Hoover often paints him as an almost untouchable figure, one who could outsmart law enforcement, rise above the violence of gang life, and ultimately become a benevolent leader advocating for the upliftment of his people. His public image, especially through the lens of the Growth and Development Movement, portrayed him as someone attempting to move his followers from a life of crime to one of self-improvement and community empowerment.

This myth was not solely cultivated by the media or the public. Many within the Gangster Disciples saw Hoover as a mentor and visionary, believing his leadership was driven by a genuine desire to help his community. For them, Hoover was not just a criminal, but a political figure whose influence extended far beyond the streets and into the realm of social justice.

The myth, however, extended even further into pop culture. In some communities, Hoover became an almost mythological figure, someone whose name was spoken with reverence, as if invoking his influence could offer protection or guarantee success. His name became synonymous with power, control, and even honor within the gang culture. This mythologizing of Hoover's persona gave him a larger-than-life status that overshadowed his actual deeds and decisions.

The Reality of Larry Hoover: The Man Behind the Myth

While the myth of Hoover as a reformer and leader holds considerable weight in certain circles, the reality of his life paints a much more complex picture. The truth of Hoover's journey cannot be fully captured by the idealized image of him as a visionary reformer or a righteous leader. To understand the reality of Larry Hoover, we must look beyond the larger-than-life narrative and examine the decisions, actions, and consequences that defined his life.

At its core, Hoover's life was marked by violence, criminality, and the trauma that often accompanies those living in poverty-stricken, marginalized communities. While Hoover did attempt to shift the GDs' focus from violence to community development, his foundation as a gang leader was built on crime, drug trafficking, and extortion. His rise to power was steeped in bloodshed, with Hoover's violent acts and criminal enterprises deeply entwined with the origins of the Gangster Disciples.

The reality of Hoover's life also reflects his incarceration and the challenges he faced in trying to separate his criminal identity from his efforts to change. Despite his attempts to distance himself from the violence of the gang, Hoover was constantly under the microscope of law enforcement, who viewed him as the central figure in a criminal network. As a result, his efforts to shift the GDs' focus toward positive growth were often overshadowed by the violent actions of his subordinates, leaving him unable to fully escape the very environment that had once nurtured his rise to power.

Furthermore, Hoover's attempts to advocate for self-improvement and community service were often hindered by the realities of prison life. While he was able to craft a message of reform, his actions remained deeply rooted in his role as a leader of a criminal enterprise. He was not able to fully transcend the life of crime that had defined him for so long, and even in his efforts to guide his followers toward self-betterment, many members of the Gangster Disciples still engaged in the illegal activities that Hoover himself had once been involved in.

The Duality of Hoover's Leadership

What stands out in the myth versus reality debate is the duality of Hoover's leadership. On the one hand, he was a criminal mastermind, orchestrating illegal activities from behind bars and maintaining a tight grip on his gang empire. On the other hand, he was a man trying to craft a new path—one that would encourage his followers to reject violence and build a better future.

In reality, Hoover's desire for a different path was stymied by his legacy as a gang leader and the inherent limitations of his environment. His transformation from a gang leader to a community advocate never fully materialized in the way he may have hoped, as his criminal activities continued to define his relationship with law enforcement and the public. Hoover's words may have advocated for growth, but the actions of his followers, often far removed from his personal ideals, continued to dominate the narrative of his life.

This duality also manifested in his relationship with the Gangster Disciples. While Hoover attempted to reframe the gang's image by promoting positive ideals, his leadership role remained deeply tied to the gang's criminal activities. The power Hoover had within the organization made it difficult to fully separate his message of growth from the ongoing criminality in the streets. For many, Hoover's name became synonymous with the gang culture—a culture that was difficult to reform from within.

Hoover's Legacy: Reformer or Kingpin?

The ultimate question regarding Hoover's legacy lies in the balance between his role as a gang leader and his efforts at personal and organizational reform. Was Larry Hoover a gang kingpin who sought to control the streets, or was he a man who tried to break free from the cycle of crime and violence that defined his early life?

The myth of Hoover, as a reformer and leader, endures in the minds of many who see him as a figure who transcended his circumstances and tried to guide others out of a life of crime. Yet, the reality of his criminal history and the ongoing operations of the GDs even during his attempts at reform paint a more complicated picture.

The reality is that Larry Hoover was a man of contradictions—someone who could simultaneously be a powerful criminal figure and a visionary reformer. His legacy, shaped by both his criminal acts and his efforts toward positive change, reflects the complexities of trying to redefine oneself within the confines of a gang culture. For many, Hoover's mythic status will always overshadow the reality of his life, but both versions are essential to understanding the full impact of his story.

Hoover's story is one of dualities, and it remains a powerful reminder of the struggle between good and evil, reform and crime, that plays out within the lives of those seeking to change their futures. His legacy will continue to be debated, but one thing remains clear—whether viewed as a reformer or a criminal mastermind, Larry Hoover has left an indelible mark on history.

Chapter 10: The Gangster Disciples Today

The Gangster Disciples (GD) are one of the most enduring and influential street organizations to ever emerge from Chicago. Founded by Larry Hoover and David Barksdale in the 1970s, the group quickly grew to dominate the South Side of Chicago, and over time, its reach spread across the United States and even internationally. While the myth of Larry Hoover's reform efforts persists, the reality is that the GDs today remain a complex, evolving entity, maintaining both criminal influence and some of the organizational structures that Hoover once hoped would serve as a force for positive change. This chapter explores the current state of the Gangster Disciples, the continuation of Hoover's legacy, and the ongoing tension between crime and reform within the group.

A Powerful Network

Today, the Gangster Disciples continue to operate as one of the largest and most influential street gangs in the world, with a presence not just in Chicago but in cities across the United States and in parts of Europe and Africa. Despite law enforcement crackdowns and Hoover's incarceration, the GDs have adapted to survive in an ever-changing environment.

The GDs maintain a hierarchical structure similar to the one Hoover established, with local chapters and various leadership roles that ensure the organization remains unified. The group is known for its discipline, loyalty, and communication strategies, which allow them to coordinate activities on a local and national scale. However, the organization's control of territories and its involvement in illegal activities, including drug trafficking, extortion, and violent crimes, has kept them under the constant scrutiny of law enforcement.

The gang's financial activities continue to drive its operations, and while Hoover's Growth and Development Movement continues to be cited in GD rhetoric, it often takes a backseat to the criminal enterprises that generate the funds needed to keep the gang's power intact. The tension between the gang's historical message of growth and its continued criminal operations has resulted in a split between members who embrace Hoover's vision of reform and those who view it as a rhetorical cover for the continuing lifestyle of violence and profit.

The Role of Larry Hoover Today

Although Larry Hoover has been incarcerated for much of the last three decades, his presence continues to loom large within the Gangster Disciples. He is regarded by many members as a godfather figure, with his ideology and teachings still central to the organization. His vision of self-improvement and community building remains part of the GD's core doctrine, but it is often overshadowed by the group's focus on maintaining power through criminal means.

For some members, Hoover's prison-based reforms were seen as a call to action, pushing them toward pursuing better lives outside of the criminal underworld. However, for others, Hoover's absence has created a power vacuum where competing factions continue to battle for control, often at the cost of the core values Hoover intended to establish. The Gangster Disciples today are caught between honoring Hoover's legacy of empowerment and embracing the harsh realities of survival within an increasingly competitive and dangerous criminal landscape.

Hoover's continuing imprisonment has allowed others within the organization, including his allies and former associates, to step into leadership roles, with some trying to steer the gang in a more positive direction. But for many, the challenge is how to balance Hoover's ideals with the reality of a gang entrenched in violence and criminality. Many still view Hoover as the ultimate authority and symbol of what the GDs could have been if the reform agenda had been fully realized.

Gangster Disciples and the Shift Toward Modern Crime

While Hoover's original goals may have leaned toward building a better community, the modern Gangster Disciples are far more involved in drug trade, extortion, and organized crime than in community service.

The structure of the gang, along with the increasing involvement of younger members, has made it harder for Hoover's original message to hold weight.

The GDs today have diversified their operations, making money not just through traditional street-level activities but also through cybercrime, money laundering, and illegal enterprises that extend beyond the traditional boundaries of gang life. The modern-day Gangster Disciples often rely on the internet to recruit new members, expand their influence, and coordinate illegal transactions, further shifting away from Hoover's ideal of using the gang for positive purposes. This transformation is indicative of how street organizations are evolving to meet the demands of a globalized, digital world.

The gang's involvement in drug trafficking remains a key part of its operations, with territories in major cities serving as lucrative hubs for the distribution of illicit substances. Chicago remains the GD's home base, but their reach extends across the U.S., from the East Coast to the West Coast, with affiliates in various parts of the country. The distribution of narcotics, including cocaine and heroin, remains one of the gang's most profitable ventures, while extortion and illegal gambling also serve as significant sources of income.

The Intersection of Community and Criminality

Despite the overwhelming dominance of criminal activities, there are still elements within the Gangster Disciples who hold on to Hoover's vision of community empowerment. Some members have attempted to create programs that focus on education, mentorship, and self-improvement for at-risk youth, often framing their efforts as a way to steer the younger generation away from crime and toward more legitimate forms of success.

These efforts are often overshadowed by the continuing cycles of violence that dominate the gang's day-to-day activities. For some, the contradictions between Hoover's message of peace and development and the gang's current operations represent an ongoing struggle within the GDs—one that has yet to find a true resolution.

There is also the question of whether the modern Gangster Disciples can still be a force for positive change when its foundational ties to violence and criminality are so deeply entrenched. While the gang does engage in various charitable and outreach activities, these efforts often feel like concessions—minor attempts to balance the dual identities of the group.

GDs in the Future: What Lies Ahead?

Looking forward, the future of the Gangster Disciples remains uncertain. The criminal underworld is constantly evolving, and the GDs are no exception. With law enforcement becoming more adept at infiltrating criminal organizations and the rise of digital crime, the GDs must either adapt to these changes or face further fragmentation and loss of influence.

In some ways, the Gangster Disciples' future may hinge on whether they can reconcile their criminal history with Hoover's ideals of growth and reform. Can the GD leadership evolve to embrace the true meaning of Hoover's vision, or will they remain trapped in cycles of crime and violence? For some, the legacy of Larry Hoover still holds the potential for reform, but for others, the gang is more about survival and power than ever before.

Ultimately, the future of the Gangster Disciples will depend on how they balance their criminal influence with their historical ties to Hoover's attempt at community rebuilding. The gang may never fully shed its criminal past, but whether or not it can successfully navigate the complexities of the modern world remains to be seen.

The Gangster Disciples today represent the evolution of a once small street organization into a vast, complex network that continues to shape both criminal activity and community culture across America. While they carry the burden of Hoover's legacy, the question remains: Will they ever truly live up to the ideals Hoover sought to establish, or will they continue to be a symbol of power, violence, and survival? Only time will tell.

Chapter 11: Calls For Freedom

As Larry Hoover's story has unfolded over the years, a persistent theme has been the call for his freedom. This call has come from various quarters—family members, former associates, activists, and even some within the public who view Hoover as a symbol of both injustice and a figure who might yet contribute to the betterment of society if given the chance. As Hoover has spent decades behind bars, his case has become a focal point for broader debates on prison reform, mass incarceration, and the possibility of redemption.

The Fight for Hoover's Release

The fight for Larry Hoover's freedom has been ongoing since his conviction in 1973, when he was sentenced to life imprisonment for his involvement in a series of crimes, including murder and the ongoing operation of the Gangster Disciples. While Hoover's actions and involvement in the gang have made his case highly controversial, there are those who argue that his sentence—which includes multiple convictions, some of which are related to actions he allegedly took while in prison—has been excessive and politically motivated.

Over the years, Hoover's supporters have consistently pushed for his release, asserting that he has undergone a profound transformation during his time in prison. Many believe that Hoover, who once espoused a message of violence and crime, has evolved into a more reflective and rehabilitated individual. His supporters argue that he has expressed remorse for his past actions and, over the course of his incarceration, has advocated for peace and community betterment, aligning with the ideals he had attempted to push for during the early days of the Growth and Development Movement.

The fight for his release has included calls for his clemency, petitions to President Obama and President Trump, and campaigns by influential individuals in the entertainment industry. Most notably, Hoover's case was brought to the forefront in 2020 when Kanye West took to social media, rallying support for Hoover's freedom in light of the broader conversation on prison reform. West, who had publicly discussed the need for criminal justice reform and the release of political prisoners, drew attention to Hoover's case as a symbol of the larger issues surrounding racial inequality and the prison system in the United States.

Arguments for Hoover's Release

Supporters of Hoover's release present several arguments to bolster their case. One key point is that Hoover has become a model prisoner, focusing on self-improvement, engaging in educational programs, and mentoring other inmates. Many point to his desire to shift away from the gang life and towards community activism as evidence that he is no longer the man he was when he first entered the prison system.

Proponents of Hoover's release also argue that his long sentence is disproportionate compared to the crimes he was convicted of. The Gangster Disciples may have been a criminal organization, but many supporters argue that Hoover's current incarceration, which stretches across multiple decades, has had a punitive rather than rehabilitative effect. Moreover, they contend that Hoover's release could serve as a powerful example of redemption, offering hope to other inmates seeking second chances after serving extended prison sentences.

Some also argue that Hoover's leadership and influence over the Gangster Disciples could be used for positive purposes if he were freed. They point to his ability to motivate and direct large numbers of people, skills that could be channeled toward addressing social issues, mentoring, and promoting peace among the youth in communities often affected by gang violence. Hoover, as the face of the GDs, could be instrumental in shifting the culture of street organizations towards more productive and law-abiding endeavors, which would be in line with the Growth and Development Movement ideals he once championed.

Opposition to Hoover's Release

While there is a vocal call for Hoover's freedom, there is also significant opposition to his release. Critics argue that Hoover's history of criminal behavior, particularly his role in directing the GDs from prison, disqualifies him from the kind of redemption his supporters believe in. Hoover's connection to violence, drug trafficking, and organized crime has left deep scars on communities, particularly in Chicago, where the Gangster Disciples wreaked havoc for decades. Many believe that Hoover's release would send the wrong message—that criminal leaders who perpetuate violence and drug-related crimes deserve leniency, even if they claim to have changed.

Opponents to Hoover's release also fear that his freedom could reignite the gang's influence. They argue that, while Hoover may have renounced violence in prison, his influence over the gang could result in a resurgence of the GDs and a return to criminal operations. His supporters may see him as a changed man, but for many law enforcement officials, his track record and the continuing criminal activity associated with his name paint a different picture. The notion that Hoover could use his position of power to promote peace among street organizations is viewed with skepticism, as there is little historical evidence to suggest that the Gangster Disciples have moved away from their criminal roots.

Furthermore, Hoover's supporters must contend with the fact that his criminal enterprise has victimized countless people over the years. The damage done by the Gangster Disciples' operations, which involved murder, drug trafficking, and extortion, is still being felt in affected communities. For those who have experienced the devastation caused by gang violence, Hoover's calls for freedom seem incongruent with the lasting harm his organization has left in its wake.

The Legal Fight

Beyond public campaigns and media attention, Hoover's legal team has worked diligently over the years to secure his release. In 1997, Hoover's attorneys filed an appeal for a new trial based on alleged misconduct during his initial trial, including claims of ineffective counsel. The appeal was unsuccessful, and Hoover's life sentence was upheld. However, his legal team continued to argue that Hoover had been unjustly convicted and that his imprisonment had gone on for far too long, considering the current state of the legal system and the fact that many of the individuals involved in similar crimes were being released due to prison reform and the changing landscape of criminal justice.

Despite the continued push for Hoover's release, his supporters face an uphill battle. Legal challenges, as well as the political and public opinion surrounding his case, have made the path to freedom a long and difficult one.

The Continuing Debate: Redemption or Danger?

Larry Hoover's case remains a divisive issue. For some, his story is a rallying cry for justice and reform, a testament to the power of personal change, growth, and second chances. To others, his release represents a dangerous misstep in a justice system that has long been criticized for its treatment of African American men, particularly those involved in gangs and organized crime.

Hoover's legacy is complicated, as it intertwines both the violent past of the Gangster Disciples and the hopeful vision of reformation that he has spoken about from his prison cell. The ongoing calls for his freedom continue to fuel this complex debate: Can Larry Hoover's life story be one of redemption? Or is the true cost of his actions still too high, despite any efforts he may have made to change?

For now, Larry Hoover remains behind bars, a prisoner of both his past actions and the current landscape of American criminal justice. His future remains uncertain, but the calls for his freedom continue to grow louder, reflecting not just on Hoover's own fate but also on the broader issues of incarceration and the possibility of true reform for those who have lived lives marked by crime and punishment.

Chapter 12: The Politics of Gang Leadership

Gang leadership, particularly within organizations like the Gangster Disciples, has always been more than just about power or control over illegal activities. It is deeply entwined with the political dynamics that govern the lives of those in the streets and the broader communities they inhabit. Larry Hoover, as the leader and figurehead of the Gangster Disciples, was not just running a criminal enterprise; he was also navigating the political landscape of Chicago's South Side, as well as the larger social environment that shaped the rise of street organizations in America.

This chapter explores the political dimensions of gang leadership, examining how figures like Hoover operate within a complex network of social influences, local governance, and even state or federal politics. From the way Hoover utilized power structures within the GDs to the manner in which he interacted with local government authorities, his leadership was shaped by political decisions and the pressures exerted by his community, law enforcement, and even public perceptions of gangs.

The Evolution of Gangs as Political Entities

While gangs have always been a presence in urban environments, the modern era saw them evolve from street crews focused mainly on localized turf wars and criminal activity to highly organized, often politically conscious entities. During the 1970s and 1980s, gang leaders, especially figures like Larry Hoover, began to recognize the potential influence they held over their communities. Instead of simply operating as criminal enterprises, gangs became more integrated into the political fabric of their surroundings.

For Hoover, gang leadership was never just about making money; it was about creating an alternative system of power, one that could rival or even surpass the political power of local authorities. The GDs, under his leadership, were not merely a criminal organization; they were a network that could mobilize youth, influence decisions, and even impact local economies. As Hoover rose to prominence, he tapped into the political void left by failing systems of governance in disadvantaged neighborhoods.

Hoover's Political Philosophy: Growth and Development

One of Hoover's most notable political maneuvers was his introduction of the Growth and Development (G.D.) Movement in the early 1980s. This initiative was aimed at steering the Gangster Disciples away from the violence and illegal activities that had been their primary means of survival. Hoover's philosophy of Growth and Development was grounded in a belief that street organizations like the GDs had the potential to become positive forces within their communities. Instead of just taking from the neighborhoods, Hoover encouraged his followers to give back, reinvest in the community, and improve the lives of residents through education, mentorship, and community service.

This was not simply an ideological shift but a strategic political move. Hoover understood that as a gang leader, his influence extended far beyond the drug trade or violent turf wars. The more the GDs were seen as community leaders working toward tangible improvements, the more political leverage they would have within their own neighborhoods. Hoover's vision for the GDs was one of empowerment, where gang members were encouraged to take on roles of leadership, not just in the streets, but also in the political landscape of their communities.

However, this philosophy also positioned Hoover as a direct challenge to the established powers within the neighborhood, police departments, and even the city government. Local officials had to contend with the fact that Hoover's organization wielded significant social influence. To some, Hoover represented a threat to the traditional power structures, as he was offering an alternative system of leadership and governance that operated outside the control of elected officials.

The Intersection of Politics and Law Enforcement

As Hoover's influence grew, so did the attention of law enforcement. Hoover's ability to operate his criminal empire from behind bars, coupled with his leadership in the Growth and Development movement, made him an even more formidable figure in the eyes of local and federal authorities. In the world of gang politics, Hoover was not only a gang leader; he was a political player, operating within a system that was constantly shifting and evolving.

The federal crackdown on the GDs was partly a result of Hoover's growing political stature. Authorities began to see the Gangster Disciples less as a local nuisance and more as a national threat that operated in multiple states. Law enforcement's understanding of Hoover shifted from seeing him simply as a criminal mastermind to viewing him as a political leader whose influence was expanding far beyond just the streets. This shift played a large role in Hoover's eventual life sentence—his capacity to rally support and gain political traction was seen as a threat to the status quo.

On the streets, the political influence of Hoover's leadership was also apparent in his relationships with local politicians. Gangs like the GDs often found themselves in situations where local political figures sought to negotiate with gang leaders for mutual benefit, whether it was in terms of community votes, peace agreements, or even public order. These relationships were often complicated by the fact that many of the individuals Hoover interacted with were trying to balance law enforcement pressures with the needs of their constituents, who were often caught in the crossfire of gang-related violence.

For Hoover, his political acumen was vital in maintaining control over his organization. It wasn't just about running the day-to-day activities of the gang; it was about creating alliances, leveraging his influence, and positioning himself as the primary decision-maker in a city where corruption, disenfranchisement, and neglect were commonplace. As the leader of one of the largest street organizations in the world, Hoover's ability to navigate the world of politics was just as important as his ability to manage the criminal side of his operation.

Political Influence and the Legacy of Larry Hoover

While Hoover's direct involvement in politics waned with his imprisonment, his influence on the politics of gang leadership continues to resonate. Modern-day gang leaders may not operate in the same way Hoover did, but they still understand the power of community control and the political leverage that comes with leading a large, organized group. Hoover's legacy within the gang world is one of political innovation, where his leadership was about more than just violence—it was about shaping the social and political landscape of his surroundings.

Today, Hoover's story is often used as a case study in the complex relationship between gangs, politics, and social change. His journey from a street hustler to a powerful political figure within the Gangster Disciples remains a reminder of how deeply politics is interwoven with the fabric of gang life. Whether seen as a hero of community empowerment or a villain of crime, Larry Hoover's role in shaping the political landscape of Chicago's South Side and beyond cannot be denied.

In the ongoing debates over criminal justice reform, gang violence, and community empowerment, Hoover's name continues to be invoked as a symbol of the intersection between gang leadership and political power. It is a complex legacy—one that leaves many wondering what could have been had Hoover been able to further his vision of a more empowered, reformed street organization.

Chapter 13: Hoover's Influence on the Next Generation

Larry Hoover's legacy as the founder of the Gangster Disciples and the leader of the Growth and Development movement has left an indelible mark on the next generation of gang leaders and members, both within the Gangster Disciples and in street organizations across the country. His influence transcends the confines of prison walls, extending far into the streets where new leaders continue to embrace his teachings, values, and political vision. This chapter explores how Hoover's leadership and philosophies have shaped the future of gang leadership and influenced the mindset of youth, both those involved in the gang life and those seeking a way out.

The Rebirth of the Gangster Disciples: A New Generation of Leadership

In the years following Hoover's imprisonment, the Gangster Disciples faced numerous challenges. While Hoover was behind bars, many of his closest allies and subordinates took up the mantle of leadership within the organization. Despite law enforcement efforts to disrupt their operations and the rise of rival gangs, Hoover's influence on the Gangster Disciples remained strong. His ideas about unity, community development, and empowerment continued to resonate with new generations of gang members.

As younger gang members rose to positions of leadership, they did so with the knowledge that Hoover's vision for the Gangster Disciples was not just about criminal activity; it was about creating a unified community and a structure of power that could rival the traditional systems in place. Hoover's teachings on self-determination and community empowerment still play a role in shaping the actions of the next generation of Gangster Disciples, even if they operate in a world that is vastly different from the one Hoover navigated in the 1970s and 1980s.

The legacy of Hoover's leadership has also contributed to the continued relevance of the Gangster Disciples in the modern street economy. The structure Hoover put in place has endured over the years, and even with the rise of newer, younger leaders, many of them still look to Hoover as an example of a powerful and respected figure who successfully navigated the world of gang politics and criminal enterprise. To this day, Hoover is often revered as the "founding father" of the modern GDs, and his role in shaping the organization continues to influence how it is structured and how it operates.

Hoover's Ideals: Growth and Development Reborn

Though Hoover's time in the streets was marked by criminal activity, his Growth and Development (G.D.) Movement has left a legacy that goes beyond crime and violence. Young people entering street organizations today are still influenced by Hoover's vision of positive change and the idea of redemption. Many leaders within gangs today continue to embrace aspects of the G.D. Movement, promoting concepts such as unity, economic self-sufficiency, and community service. While the day-to-day activities of street organizations may still involve violence and illicit trade, Hoover's political and social philosophies provide an ideological framework that motivates those seeking something more than just crime.

For younger gang members, Hoover's vision of community reinvestment, education, and empowerment has had a profound impact on how they view their role within their neighborhoods. Many are drawn to his message of growth, not just in terms of personal success, but as a community-wide push for progress and unity. Even as the criminal side of the Gangster Disciples endures, there is an undercurrent of those seeking to live up to Hoover's vision of improvement, creating a legacy of hope amid the despair of gang violence.

In some cases, Hoover's ideas on leadership and social responsibility have even inspired former gang members to seek alternatives to the street life. Community leaders and activists, who were once part of the Gangster Disciples, are now working to reshape the lives of youth and offer mentorship, job training, and educational programs as an alternative to joining gangs. These individuals, many of whom were influenced by Hoover's teachings, have become key players in the fight against violence and the quest for positive change.

The Gangster Disciples: An Ever-Evolving Movement

Larry Hoover's influence, however, is not solely confined to those who follow his principles in the most idealistic sense. The gang world is inherently fluid, and the Gangster Disciples have evolved with the times. New generations of gang members often adapt Hoover's ideas to their own realities, sometimes distorting or reinterpreting his philosophy to suit their needs. For some, Hoover represents a symbol of power and respect, and his vision is used as a tool for gaining influence rather than as a means of social reform.

For example, some younger leaders have taken Hoover's idea of empowerment and applied it in a way that strengthens their positions of dominance within the gang hierarchy. They use his Growth and Development movement as a foundation for financial gain and territorial control, rather than community growth or youth mentorship. In this way, Hoover's ideals have been co-opted by those who view the gang life through a more self-interested lens, rather than as a platform for larger social change.

Despite these variations, Hoover's original vision continues to inspire significant portions of gang leaders who aim to bring about a better life for their communities. Whether these ideals are practiced in their most authentic form or are reinterpreted to suit contemporary realities, Larry Hoover's teachings remain a defining force in the ongoing evolution of gang culture.

The Continued Appeal of Hoover's Legacy

Larry Hoover's influence extends beyond the Gangster Disciples. Many gangs around the country, even outside of Chicago, have taken cues from his style of leadership, his ideas about organization, and his method of creating community-based power structures. Hoover's story has become one of both inspiration and caution, representing the potential for positive change in gang leadership, while also illustrating the dangerous consequences of intertwining politics and criminal enterprise.

For today's youth, the story of Larry Hoover provides an example of resilience, strategic thinking, and unwavering determination. His rise to power—despite the odds stacked against him—serves as a blueprint for those who are seeking to make something of themselves, whether in the streets or in more legitimate spheres of society. Hoover's influence remains powerful because it speaks to the aspirations of young people who feel marginalized, disenfranchised, and disconnected from the structures of power in society.

In a broader sense, Hoover's legacy is intertwined with the ongoing battle for social justice and reform. His influence on the next generation reflects the need for alternatives to the gang life, as well as the continuing struggle for youth empowerment and social change. As long as the lessons of Growth and Development resonate, Hoover's impact will continue to shape the future of gang culture, for better or worse.

A Complex Legacy

While Hoover's influence remains a driving force in many aspects of gang leadership, it is important to remember the complexity of his legacy. On one hand, Hoover's vision for community growth and his desire to build an alternative system of empowerment continue to inspire the next generation of gang leaders, community activists, and reformers. On the other hand, the criminal nature of his organization and the violent tactics employed by many within the Gangster Disciples complicate the narrative of Hoover's legacy.

The next generation of gang members, whether they continue Hoover's vision for empowerment or choose to exploit it for personal gain, will always be shaped by the story of Larry Hoover. His influence, both positive and negative, continues to guide and challenge the youth of today, leaving them with an undeniable question: What will be their legacy?

Chapter 14: What If?

In exploring the life of Larry Hoover, the Gangster Disciples, and their complex impact on American society, one question that often arises is the hypothetical: What if things had gone differently? This chapter seeks to examine alternative outcomes in Hoover's life and the broader ramifications for the gang culture he helped shape, the criminal justice system, and even the communities affected by his organization. By asking "what if," we not only consider the potential shifts in Hoover's life path but also reflect on the broader social dynamics, asking how different decisions might have led to a different legacy.

What if Larry Hoover Had Never Gone to Prison?

One of the most significant turning points in Larry Hoover's life was his imprisonment in 1973. If Hoover had never been incarcerated, how might his life—and the trajectory of the Gangster Disciples—have unfolded?

Without prison, Hoover would likely have retained control over the Gangster Disciples during a critical time in the gang's rise to prominence. He was already a charismatic and strategic leader, and his ability to organize and maintain loyalty within the gang could have propelled the Growth and Development movement further, influencing even more communities. It's possible that Hoover might have leveraged his leadership and resources to build businesses, further invest in community development, or even become a prominent figure in the local political landscape.

However, the absence of his prison sentence may have also meant that Hoover's gang could have grown in power and scope, with less oversight from law enforcement and other competing gangs. This could have led to more violent clashes, territorial disputes, and an even more entrenched position in the criminal underworld.

Ultimately, Hoover's incarceration created an opportunity for him to distance himself from the criminal operations and become a symbol of reform and resilience—a narrative that still fuels much of his legacy today.

What if the Growth and Development Movement Had Gained Nationwide Attention?

The Growth and Development (G.D.) Movement, as an ideology, provided an alternative vision for gang members—a vision rooted in empowerment, self-sufficiency, and community betterment. If Hoover's message had gained greater traction during the height of his influence, could it have led to gang reform on a broader scale?

What if communities had fully embraced Hoover's philosophy of unity, economic development, and education? What if, instead of falling deeper into crime, young people in gang-affiliated areas across the U.S. had sought legitimate opportunities for success, propelled by Hoover's alternative narrative?

Had Hoover's ideas been better supported or more widely implemented, it could have transformed how gangs were viewed in society—shifting the conversation from criminality to community empowerment. The G.D. Movement might have even paved the way for a nationwide effort to reduce gang violence through economic development programs, youth mentoring, and leadership training. In essence, Hoover could have become a figure of reform, like a modern-day activist and community organizer, pushing back against the tide of systemic poverty and disenfranchisement.

What if the U.S. Government Had Embraced Rehabilitation Over Punishment?

Another key "what if" scenario is the treatment of Larry Hoover by the U.S. criminal justice system. Hoover's life sentence and the way in which he was treated while incarcerated speak to larger questions about the effectiveness of the U.S. prison system. What if the criminal justice system had placed more emphasis on rehabilitation instead of long-term punitive measures?

Had Hoover been offered more opportunities for rehabilitation, education, and meaningful reintegration into society, it's possible that he could have become a true advocate for change, not just a figurehead of a gang. His organizational skills, leadership capabilities, and ability to influence large groups could have been channeled into positive community-building efforts. Hoover's voice could have resonated not only in the streets but also in the halls of government and politics, potentially leading to real policy changes focused on prison reform, gang intervention, and community empowerment.

However, the reality of the U.S. penal system's approach to gangs—focused on isolation, punishment, and incapacitation—has kept Hoover within the confines of incarceration rather than leveraging his leadership for societal benefit. This lack of rehabilitation opportunities has left many to wonder if a different approach could have resulted in a better outcome for Hoover, the Gangster Disciples, and the broader community.

What if Larry Hoover Had Become a Political Leader?

As one of the most well-known gang figures in American history, Larry Hoover had the potential to influence not only his followers but also the broader public perception of street organizations. His ability to organize, his political acumen, and his message of empowerment were not solely limited to the criminal world. What if Hoover had taken his vision to the political sphere and sought to reform communities in a way that brought about systemic change?

Had Hoover pivoted from the streets to the political stage, he might have been able to advocate for meaningful reforms in neighborhoods plagued by violence, poverty, and crime. Hoover's political agenda could have involved building better schools, creating job opportunities, and fostering stronger community relations with law enforcement. He may have gained national attention, not as a criminal figure, but as an influential leader with the power to bring about change.

It's worth noting that such a shift would have likely faced immense resistance, both from the government and from other gang figures who saw Hoover's political ambitions as a threat to their power. However, had he been able to successfully navigate these challenges, Hoover could have become a transformational leader, not only for his followers but for marginalized communities nationwide.

What if the Gangster Disciples Had Embraced Full Reform?

Finally, what if the Gangster Disciples—under Hoover's leadership—had embraced a full-scale reform of their operations, focusing entirely on community development rather than criminal enterprise? Hoover's philosophy of growth and development held the potential for lasting change, but it is often overshadowed by the criminal aspect of the gang's operations.

Had Hoover and his followers fully transitioned from the criminal underworld to legitimate businesses, social services, or political advocacy, the Gangster Disciples could have become a positive force in society. They could have invested in local economies, funded community organizations, and worked alongside social activists to push for a better future for disenfranchised youth.

Such a radical shift would have required a monumental effort, both within the gang and in broader society. But the question remains: What if the Gangster Disciples had embraced that shift? Could they have been a force for good, creating a model of gang transformation that might have influenced similar organizations across the country?

The Power of "What If"

The question of "what if" allows us to reflect on the complexities of Larry Hoover's life and legacy. It challenges us to consider alternative outcomes and the broader impact of his decisions, both on his life and on the lives of those who followed him. While we can never truly know how things might have turned out differently, asking these questions helps us understand the broader implications of leadership, power, and reform—both in the world of gangs and in society at large.

In the end, what if is not just about speculation or regret; it is about recognizing the potential for change and the importance of leadership, even in the most difficult and trying circumstances. It is a reminder that the choices we make, both individually and collectively, shape the world we live in—just as Hoover's choices have shaped the future of gang culture and community reform in the U.S.

Chapter 15: Legacy of a Street General

Larry Hoover, a name synonymous with the Gangster Disciples and the broader landscape of urban gang culture, has left a profound and lasting legacy that continues to influence various realms of American society, from the streets to the criminal justice system. But his legacy, much like his life, is complex, controversial, and multifaceted—provoking deep reflections on the nature of leadership, survival, and reform.

In this final chapter, we will explore the legacy of Larry Hoover, how his actions shaped gang culture, his role as a street general, and the lasting influence he has on both society at large and the communities he once sought to control.

The Legacy of Leadership

At the core of Larry Hoover's legacy lies his unquestionable leadership. Whether through his rise from humble beginnings to becoming the head of one of the largest street organizations in the U.S., or his ability to maintain control while incarcerated, Hoover's skill as a strategist and organizer is undeniable. His leadership style transcended mere criminal activities; it resonated with principles of order, discipline, and loyalty, all vital traits for anyone leading a large group.

As a street general, Hoover commanded respect not only from his fellow gang members but also from his adversaries and even the broader criminal world. His leadership extended beyond typical gang activities, influencing how his followers viewed loyalty, self-improvement, and unity. Under Hoover's guidance, the Gangster Disciples went from a local Chicago-based gang to a national presence, and his ability to shape the organization's culture through the Growth and Development movement remains one of his most transformational impacts.

However, Hoover's influence was not just about the power dynamics of gangs but also about how street leaders and criminals can leverage their positions for economic gain, political influence, and even social change. While many viewed Hoover as a villain, others saw him as an unconventional leader who managed to galvanize thousands of people to follow him and maintain a sense of unity and purpose, albeit within a controversial and often destructive context.

Gang Culture and Its Lasting Impact

The Gangster Disciples are a symbol of gang culture across the U.S., and much of that culture was shaped by Hoover's leadership. His influence extended beyond violence and criminal enterprise; he also introduced the idea that gangs could serve as a means of survival, protection, and community for those living in poverty-stricken neighborhoods.

The hierarchical structure Hoover established within the Gangster Disciples created a level of organization and discipline that many street organizations lacked. This structure not only made the gang more formidable but also solidified Hoover's place as a central figure in the realm of street politics. His emphasis on the concept of the Six-Point Star and the principles of Growth and Development has been a focal point for how modern gangs and street organizations can evolve beyond violence and find unity through solidarity and self-improvement.

Hoover's teachings continue to permeate gang culture, influencing younger generations of gang members and the direction of street organizations in ways both positive and negative. His ability to shape such a culture, where rules and organization could exist in such a turbulent environment, has made him a legend—both feared and respected—among those in the streets.

The Criminal Justice System and the Battle for Freedom

While Hoover's influence within the gang world is undeniable, his relationship with the criminal justice system has been one of the most significant elements of his legacy. His life sentence for crimes related to the Gangster Disciples and his years spent in prison have ignited discussions about the effectiveness of the prison system, the treatment of incarcerated individuals, and the societal implications of punishment versus rehabilitation.

As Hoover remains imprisoned, his supporters continue to advocate for his release, citing his role as an agent of change and a reformer who could influence positive outcomes if given the opportunity. While many still view him as a criminal mastermind, others argue that Hoover's transformation from a gang leader to a voice of reform in the community speaks to the possibility of redemption.

Hoover's ongoing incarceration has raised questions about the broader injustices within the criminal justice system, particularly in how it deals with individuals who show signs of rehabilitation or those whose influence might be used for greater societal benefit. His supporters maintain that Hoover's release would allow him to continue the mission of community upliftment and provide a model for others in similar situations, showing that leadership, even if initially born in criminality, can evolve into something greater for society.

The Ongoing Debate: Hero or Villain?

At the heart of Hoover's legacy lies the ongoing debate about his moral standing. To some, he is a hero, a figure who transcended the violence and despair of the streets to become an advocate for growth and development. To others, he remains a villain, a criminal whose legacy is intertwined with violence, manipulation, and the perpetuation of gang culture.

His transformation from a ruthless gang leader to a proponent of positive change makes Hoover's legacy all the more complex. He may not have achieved the redemption he sought in life, but his words and influence continue to resonate with individuals caught in the cycle of poverty, crime, and systemic disenfranchisement.

In the end, Hoover's legacy is a study in contradictions—a story of a man who shaped a culture, defied odds, and redefined leadership in the streets. Whether seen as a villain or a visionary, his impact is undeniable, and his story is a reflection of the larger societal issues that many still face today.

Hoover's Impact on the Next Generation

Larry Hoover's influence extends far beyond his own era. Generations of young men and women who grew up in neighborhoods dominated by gangs have looked to Hoover, whether consciously or subconsciously, as a model of how to wield power, gain respect, and navigate the harsh realities of life. Even as the Gangster Disciples evolve, Hoover's legacy serves as a touchstone for those seeking purpose, respect, and survival.

The next generation of street leaders has adopted elements of Hoover's approach to gang politics, from the organizational structure to the sense of belonging that it offers to marginalized youth. Despite Hoover's imprisonment, his ideology and methods still resonate with young people who find themselves caught between the promise of a better future and the harsh realities of street life.

As Hoover's story unfolds, new voices emerge, inspired by his example, yet seeking to carve their own path and make their own choices. The struggle for identity, self-determination, and freedom that Hoover faced is now the struggle of a new generation, who continue to debate the impact of Hoover's legacy and whether his vision will be realized on their terms.

Conclusion: A Street General's Enduring Legacy

Larry Hoover's legacy, as a street general, leader of the Gangster Disciples, and proponent of growth, development, and change, will undoubtedly continue to be a subject of intense debate for years to come. Whether admired or vilified, Hoover's place in the tapestry of American criminal history is cemented, and his influence—both positive and negative—has shaped the landscape of gang culture, prison reform, and even political discourse.

In the end, Hoover's legacy is one of complexity and contradiction—a reminder that leadership, whether good or bad, can leave a lasting imprint on society and the generations that follow. His story serves as both a cautionary tale and a source of inspiration, demonstrating the immense power of a single individual to shape a movement, change lives, and leave an indelible mark on history.

Afterword: A Call for His Release

As we conclude the exploration of Larry Hoover's life and legacy, it's impossible to ignore the ongoing conversation surrounding his incarceration and the call for his release. While Hoover's past is marred by his leadership of a criminal organization and the crimes he committed, his transformation over the years, his advocacy for reform, and his commitment to community betterment warrant a closer look at the possibility of his release.

Throughout this narrative, we've seen that Hoover's evolution from a gang leader to a proponent of growth and development demonstrates the potential for rehabilitation in even the most difficult circumstances. His teachings, while controversial, include messages of discipline, self-improvement, and positive change—values that have inspired many individuals to change their lives, even from within the walls of prison.

Hoover's journey isn't just one of crime and punishment, but also one of redemption. Over the years, he has shown an ability to use his voice and position, even from behind bars, to inspire others to seek a better way of life. He has reached the hearts of many who have been trapped in cycles of poverty and violence and has given them the tools to break free. If given the opportunity, Hoover's influence could be used for even greater good, not only within his community but for society at large.

The criminal justice system is built on the principle of rehabilitation. While some may argue that Hoover's past actions disqualify him from this chance, the reality is that many individuals who have committed serious offenses have been given second chances. Hoover has served over four decades of incarceration, and during that time, he has demonstrated an unwavering commitment to self-reflection, growth, and reform. His supporters argue that the time has come for Hoover to be allowed to make a real difference in society outside the prison walls.

For years, Hoover has been a symbol of hope to those who believed that their circumstances defined their future. His rise from the streets to the leader of a national organization was a testament to the power of resilience and leadership. Now, as a prisoner, he continues to embody the hope that change is possible, even for those who have made the most mistakes. The call for Hoover's release isn't about ignoring his past but recognizing the person he has become and his ability to contribute to society in a meaningful and positive way.

It is time to look beyond the man Larry Hoover once was and to embrace the potential of the man he is now. Hoover's voice has been a source of inspiration for many, and it could be a force for good if given the chance to impact the broader world.

This afterword is not just a call for Hoover's release—it is a call for a reexamination of the criminal justice system's approach to rehabilitation. It is a reminder that people change, and that true redemption should be valued as much as punishment. Larry Hoover has shown that even in the darkest places, the seeds of growth, reform, and leadership can take root. It is time to give him the opportunity to fully live out his legacy—not as a figure of the past, but as a voice of change for the future.

It's time to call for his release—not as a free pass, but as a chance for redemption, a chance to continue his journey of growth, and a chance to prove that even the most difficult pasts can be transformed into something powerful for the greater good of society. Larry Hoover's story is far from over, and it is time for a new chapter—one where he can live, lead, and inspire without the confines of prison.

Also by Jonah Sanders

Black Genius Academy
A Deep Dive Into Nouns : A Beginner Study To All Forms of Nouns
A Journey To The Solar System : A Elementary Study On The Solar System

The Genius Guide
How To Start A LLC
Fundamentals of Banking
Common Criminal Law Defense's
The History of Religion
Fundamentals of Real Estate
Fundamentals of Conflict Resolution
Parenting 101

The Law With Jonah Sanders
The Law With Jonah Sanders: Incompetency to Stand Trial
The Law With Jonah Sanders: Prosecutorial Misconduct
The Law With Jonah Sanders: Ineffective Assistance of Counsel
The Law With Jonah Sanders: Habeas Corpus Guide
The Law With Jonah Sanders: Prisoner Rights

The Urban Law School
Prison. Parole. Redemption: A Deeper Look
Murder On The Mind: A Review On Murder, The Psychology and Criminal Defense
So...The United States Constitution?: A Review of Each Amendment
Unzipping The Mind: The Psychology of Criminal Minds

Standalone
The Message To The Black Man In America 2.0
The Not Sweet 16: 16 Supreme Court Cases That Affected Black People
66 Hadith's For The Newly Converted Muslim
A Guide To Common Types of Mental Health Disorders
3 Great Dangers:. Examining Anger, Anxiety & Backbiting
Being True To Christ: Examining Forgiveness, Mercy & Repentance
Math For Toddlers
Number Time: Number Tracing
Sketching Lines & Shapes
Tracing & Coloring Animals
Tracing & Writing Letters
The Pig
Think You Can Get It? A Book of Riddles
And Soon They'll Be Men: Raising Black Boys
This Is Islam: A Simple Guide To The Teachings Of The Religion
The Art of Gangbanging: A Review on Gang Culture
Common Criminal Defenses
30 Juz of Quran: A Guide For New Muslims
Black Love? Topics That Black People Need To Discuss
Rise Young King: Lessons For Young Black Boys
Ending Human Trafficking : What Everyone Should Know

The Art of Being Solid: Lessons On Life And Reality
Audi, Vide, Tace: A Companion Guide To Freemasonry
The Gang Bible: A Review On The Most Dangerous Street Gangs
The Message For Black Women
I Was You: A Message For At-Risk Youth
Outside My Project Window
Only One Christ: A Review of Christian Denominations
A Comprehensive Guide To Prisoners Rights
So...I'm Your Nigga: A Collection of Poetry
For My Mother
The Book of Samuels: Kevin Samuels Guide For High-Value Men
The Miseducation of Jonah Sanders: A Collection of Poetry and Thoughts
Lion of Allah: The Life & Legacy of Minister Louis Farrakhan
"Street Shadows: The Rise of Gangs in Newark and New Jersey"
Mother Africa: The History of the Colonization of Africa
Black, Gangster, & Respected: The Larry Hoover Story
Sexyy Red, Frequencies & The Agenda of The Hip-hop Industry
Before The Slave Trade: Proof That Black People Have Been In America
The Origin and Evolution of " Nigger ": A History of Power, Pain, and Progression
Even A Black Man Cries

Watch for more at jonahsanders.com.

About the Author

Jonah Sanders is a renowned educator, author, poet and overall Renaissance Man. He is the founder of Genius IQ and The Urban Law School.

Read more at https://www.iamjonahsanders.com/.